The Four Functions of Principle Management

A Practical Guide to Leadership and Decision-Making

James Grell

Copyright © James Grell 2023
All Rights Reserved

Table of contents

Chapter One 2
Chapter Two 2
Planning for Success 2
Chapter Three 2
Organizing for Efficiency 2
Chapter Four 2
Leading with Influence 2
Chapter Five 2
Controlling for Results 2
Chapter Six 2
Planning for the Future 2
Chapter Seven 2
Organizing for Growth 2
Chapter Eight 2
Leading in a Diverse World 2
Chapter Nine 2
Managing Change 2
Chapter Conclusion 2

Ethics and Social Responsibility 2
Introduction 1

Introduction

"Welcome to 'The Four Functions of Principle Management: A Practical Guide to Leadership and Decision-Making.' In this book, we will explore the four key principles that form the foundation of effective management: planning, organizing, leading, and controlling. These functions are essential for any manager or leader seeking to achieve success in today's fast-paced, constantly changing business environment.

Throughout this book, we will delve into each of these functions in-depth, providing practical tips and real-world examples of how to apply them in a variety of organizational settings. We will also discuss the challenges that managers and leaders face in executing these functions and offer strategies for overcoming those challenges.

Whether you are a seasoned manager looking to refine your skills or a new leader just starting on your management journey, this book will provide valuable insights and guidance to help you navigate the complexities of modern business. So let's get started on exploring the four functions of management and how they can help you become a more effective and successful leader."

"In the world of business, there are few things more important than effective management. At its core, management is about maximizing the potential of a team or organization by setting clear goals, creating a plan for achieving those goals, and executing that plan with efficiency and precision. It is about inspiring and motivating others to perform at their best, and about making tough decisions that drive progress and success.

But being a successful manager is not always easy. It requires a unique combination of skills, including the ability to think strategically, communicate effectively, delegate tasks, and solve problems. It also requires a deep understanding of the principles that underpin good management, such as the four functions we will explore in this book: planning, organizing, leading, and controlling.

By mastering these functions, you can not only improve your performance as a manager but also create a more positive and productive work environment for your team. So if you're ready to take your management skills to the next level, this book is for you. Let's dive in and explore the principles that will help you become a more effective and successful leader."

Chapter One

In this chapter, we will introduce the four key principles of management: planning, organizing, leading, and controlling. These functions form the foundation of effective management and are essential for any manager or leader seeking to achieve success in today's fast-paced, constantly changing business environment.
1.1 The Importance of Management.
Management is the process of achieving organizational goals through the effective use of resources. This includes everything from setting clear goals and creating a plan for achieving them to inspiring and motivating a team, monitoring progress, and making

adjustments as needed to ensure that goals are being met. Good management is essential for the success of any team or organization, as it helps to maximize efficiency, productivity, and profitability.

1.2 The Four Functions of Management.

The four functions of management are the key principles that underlie effective management. These functions are:

Planning: This involves setting clear goals and creating a roadmap for achieving them. Planning includes activities such as setting targets, conducting a SWOT analysis to identify strengths, weaknesses, opportunities, and threats, and allocating resources to support the plan.

Organizing: This involves structuring a team or organization in a way that maximizes efficiency and effectiveness. Organizing includes activities such as departmentalization, a span of control, and centralization vs. decentralization.

Leading: This involves inspiring and motivating others to perform at their best. Leading includes activities such as communication, delegation, and conflict resolution.

Controlling: This involves monitoring progress and making adjustments as needed to ensure that goals are being met. Controlling includes activities such as setting performance metrics, providing feedback, and taking corrective action when needed.

1.3 The Interdependence of the Four Functions.

It is important to note that the four functions of management are interdependent, meaning that they all work together to create a cohesive, effective management approach. For example, effective planning is necessary for successful organizing, leading, and controlling. Similarly, strong leadership is essential for effective planning, organizing, and controlling.

1.4 The Role of the Manager.

The role of the manager is to effectively execute the four functions of management to achieve organizational goals. This requires a combination of technical skills (such as the ability to analyze data and make informed decisions) and interpersonal skills (such as the ability to communicate and build strong relationships).

1.5 Conclusion

In summary, the four functions of management - planning, organizing, leading, and controlling - are the key principles that form the foundation of effective management. In the following chapters, we will delve into each of these functions in more detail and provide practical tips and real-world examples of how to apply them in a variety of organizational settings.

Chapter Two

Planning for Success

In this chapter, we will explore the importance of planning in management and discuss strategies for setting clear goals and creating a roadmap for achieving them.

2.1 The Importance of Planning

Planning is a crucial function of management, as it helps to ensure that an organization is working towards clear, achievable goals. By setting targets and creating a plan for achieving them, managers can maximize efficiency, minimize waste, and increase the chances of success. Planning also helps to identify potential challenges and opportunities and create a strategy for dealing with them.

2.2 Types of Planning

There are several types of planning that managers can use, including:

Strategic planning: This involves setting long-term goals and creating a roadmap for achieving them. It involves analyzing the organization's strengths, weaknesses, opportunities, and threats (SWOT analysis) and creating a plan that aligns with the organization's overall vision and mission.

Operational planning: This involves creating a plan for the day-to-day activities of the organization. It includes setting targets, allocating resources, and creating procedures for achieving specific objectives.

Contingency planning: This involves creating a plan for dealing with unexpected events or situations. It includes identifying potential risks and creating a strategy for responding to them.

2.3 Steps in the Planning Process

There are several steps involved in the planning process, including:

Setting goals: The first step in planning is to identify clear, measurable goals that align with the organization's overall vision and mission.

Conducting a SWOT analysis: Next, it is important to conduct a SWOT analysis to identify the organization's strengths, weaknesses, opportunities, and threats. This will help to inform the planning process and identify potential challenges and opportunities.

Allocating resources: Once the goals and potential challenges and opportunities have been identified, it is important to allocate the necessary resources to support the plan. This includes things like personnel, funding, and equipment.

Creating a roadmap: With the goals and resources in place, the next step is to create a roadmap for achieving those goals. This should include specific tasks and milestones, as well as a timeline for completing them.

2.4 Challenges in Planning

There are several challenges that managers may face in the planning process, including:

Lack of resources: Limited resources can make it difficult to achieve certain goals. It may be necessary to prioritize certain goals over others or to identify alternative ways of achieving them.

Changing circumstances: The business environment is constantly changing, and this can make it difficult to create a long-term plan that remains relevant. Managers need to be flexible and willing to adjust their plans as needed in response to changing circumstances.

Resistance to change: When creating a new plan, it is common for team members to resist change. It is important for managers to communicate the benefits of the plan and to involve team members in the planning process to help mitigate this resistance.

2.5 Conclusion

In summary, planning is a crucial function of management that helps to ensure that an organization is working towards clear, achievable goals. It involves setting targets, conducting a SWOT analysis, allocating resources, and creating a roadmap for achieving those goals. While there are challenges in the planning process, effective planning can help to maximize efficiency, minimize waste, and increase the chances of success.

Chapter Three

Organizing for Efficiency

In this chapter, we will discuss the importance of organizing in management and explore strategies for structuring a team or organization in a way that maximizes efficiency and effectiveness.

3.1 The Importance of Organizing.

Organizing is a crucial function of management, as it involves creating a structure for a team or organization that enables it to achieve its goals efficiently and effectively. A well-organized team or organization can use its resources effectively and minimize waste, resulting in increased productivity and profitability.

3.2 Elements of Organizing

There are several key elements to consider when organizing a team or organization, including:

Departmentalization: This involves grouping activities into departments based on function, product, customer, or geographic location. This helps to clarify roles and responsibilities and makes it easier to coordinate and manage activities.

The span of control: This refers to the number of subordinates that a manager is responsible for overseeing. A narrow span of control means that a manager has a smaller number of subordinates, while a wide span of control means that a manager has a larger number of subordinates. The appropriate span of control will depend on factors such as the complexity of the work and the experience and capabilities of the manager.

Centralization vs. decentralization: Centralization refers to decision-making power being concentrated at the top levels of an organization, while decentralization refers to decision-making power being distributed throughout the organization. The appropriate approach will depend on factors such as the size and complexity of the organization, as well as the expertise and capabilities of employees.

3.3 Challenges in Organizing

There are several challenges that managers may face when organizing a team or organization, including:

Resource constraints: Limited resources can make it difficult to create an effective organizational structure. It may be necessary to prioritize certain activities or to find creative solutions to resource constraints.

Communication issues: Poor communication can hinder the effectiveness of an organizational structure. It is important to establish clear channels of communication and to ensure that all team members are aware of their roles and responsibilities.

Resistance to change: When implementing a new organizational structure, it is common for team members to resist change. It is important for managers to communicate the benefits of the new structure and to involve team members in the process to help mitigate this resistance.

3.4 Conclusion

In summary, organizing is a crucial function of management that involves creating a structure for a team or organization that enables it to achieve its goals efficiently and effectively. Key elements of organizing include departmentalization, a span of control, and centralization vs. decentralization. While there are challenges in organizing, a well-organized team or organization can use its resources effectively and minimize waste, resulting in increased productivity and profitability.

Chapter Four

Leading with Influence

In this chapter, we will explore the role of leadership in management and discuss strategies for inspiring and motivating others.

4.1 The Importance of Leadership.

Leadership is a crucial function of management, as it involves inspiring and motivating others to perform at their best. A good leader can create a positive, productive work environment, build strong relationships with team members, and foster a sense of shared purpose and vision.

4.2 Styles of Leadership.

There are several styles of leadership that managers can use, including:

Authoritative: This style involves a leader taking a strong, decisive approach and giving clear direction to team members. It is effective in situations where there is a need for quick decision-making or when there is a clear vision that needs to be implemented.

Participative: This style involves a leader involving team members in the decision-making process and seeking their input and feedback. It is effective in situations where team members have valuable expertise or where the buy-in is needed for a particular course of action.

Coaching: This style involves a leader providing guidance and support to team members to help them develop their skills and achieve their potential. It is effective in situations where team members need support and development to reach their goals.

Laissez-faire: This style involves a leader taking a hands-off approach and giving team members a high degree of autonomy. It is effective in situations where team members have a high level of expertise and can work effectively without close supervision.

4.3 Challenges in Leading.

There are several challenges that managers may face when leading a team, including:

Resistance to change: When implementing a new course of action or making changes to established processes, it is common for team members to resist. It is important for leaders to communicate the benefits of the change and to involve team members in the process to help mitigate this resistance.

Communication issues: Poor communication can hinder a leader's ability to effectively motivate and inspire team members. It is important for leaders to establish clear channels of communication and to be transparent and open in their communication.

Differing motivations: Team members may have different motivations and goals, which can make it challenging for a leader to effectively inspire and motivate them. It is important for leaders to understand the needs and motivations of their team members and to tailor their leadership approach accordingly.

4.4 Conclusion

In summary, leadership is a crucial function of management that involves inspiring and motivating others to perform at their best. There are several styles of leadership that managers can use, including authoritative, participative, coaching, and laissez-faire. While there are challenges in leading, a good leader can create a positive, productive work environment, build strong relationships with team members, and foster a sense of shared purpose and vision.

Chapter Five

Controlling for Results

In this chapter, we will discuss the importance of controlling management and explore strategies for monitoring progress and making adjustments as needed to ensure that goals are being met.

5.1 The Importance of Controlling.

Controlling is a crucial function of management, as it involves monitoring progress and making adjustments as needed to ensure that goals are being met. By setting performance metrics and regularly reviewing them, managers can identify areas for improvement and take corrective action when necessary. This helps to maximize efficiency, productivity, and profitability.

5.2 Steps in the Controlling Process.

There are several steps involved in the controlling process, including:

Setting performance metrics: The first step in controlling is to establish clear, measurable performance metrics that align with the organization's goals. This may include things like sales targets, customer satisfaction scores, or productivity levels.

Monitoring progress: Once the performance metrics have been

set, it is important to regularly monitor progress to ensure that goals are being met. This may involve collecting and analyzing data, such as sales figures or customer feedback.

Providing feedback: Regular feedback is an important part of the controlling process. By providing team members with regular, constructive feedback, managers can help them understand their strengths and areas for improvement and encourage them to continue to develop

Chapter Six

Planning for the Future

In this chapter, we will discuss how managers can use forecasting techniques to anticipate and prepare for future challenges and opportunities.

6.1 The Importance of Planning for the Future

In today's fast-paced, constantly changing business environment, it is more important than ever for organizations to be proactive in their planning. By anticipating and preparing for future challenges and opportunities, organizations can stay ahead of the curve and position themselves for success.

6.2 Forecasting Techniques.

There are several forecasting techniques that managers can use to anticipate and prepare for the future, including:

Market research: By gathering and analyzing data on market trends, customer preferences, and competitors, managers can gain a better understanding of the current market landscape and anticipate future developments.

Trend analysis: By examining trends in data, such as sales figures or customer feedback, managers can identify patterns and make predictions about future developments.

Scenario planning: This involves creating multiple possible scenarios for the future and developing a plan for each one.

This helps organizations to be more resilient and adaptable in the face of uncertainty.

6.3 Challenges in Planning for the Future.

There are several challenges that managers may face when planning for the future, including:

Lack of data: It can be difficult to make accurate predictions if there is a lack of data or if the data is of poor quality. Managers need to gather and analyze as much.

Chapter Seven

Organizing for Growth

In this chapter, we will explore how managers can structure and reorganize their teams or organizations to support expansion and scalability.

7.1 The Importance of Organizing for Growth.

As organizations grow and evolve, their structure and organization need to be able to support that growth. By anticipating and preparing for expansion, organizations can ensure that they can take advantage of new opportunities and remain competitive.

7.2 Restructuring

One way for managers to support growth is to restructure their teams or organizations. This may involve reorganizing departments, changing the span of control, or centralizing or decentralizing decision-making. Restructuring can help to streamline processes, increase efficiency, and better align the organization with its goals.

7.3 Mergers and Acquisitions.

Another way for organizations to support growth is through mergers and acquisitions. By acquiring other businesses or merging with them, organizations can expand their market presence, access new resources and expertise, and increase their competitiveness.

7.4 Global Expansion.

For organizations looking to expand beyond their domestic market, global expansion can be a viable option. This may involve setting up operations in new countries or regions, entering into partnerships or joint ventures with local organizations, or licensing products or services.

7.5 Challenges in Organizing for Growth.

There are several challenges that managers may face when organizing for growth, including:

Resource constraints: Expanding an organization can be resource-intensive, and it may be necessary to prioritize certain activities or to find creative solutions to resource constraints.

Cultural differences: When expanding into new markets, it is important to consider cultural differences and to adapt business practices and communication styles accordingly.

Regulatory issues: Different countries and regions may have

different regulations and compliance requirements, and organizations need to be aware of and adhere to these requirements when expanding globally.

7.6 Conclusion

In summary, organizing for growth is an important aspect of management that involves anticipating and preparing for expansion and scalability. This may involve restructuring, pursuing mergers and acquisitions, or expanding globally. While there are challenges in organizing for growth, it can help organizations too.

Chapter Eight

Leading in a Diverse World

In this chapter, we will discuss the importance of diversity and inclusion in management and explore strategies for leading and managing a diverse team.

8.1 The Importance of Diversity and Inclusion.

Diversity and inclusion are crucial for the success of any organization. A diverse team brings a range of perspectives, experiences, and skills that can lead to better decision-making, increased creativity and innovation, and improved performance. Inclusion, on the other hand, involves creating an environment where all team members feel valued, respected, and able to contribute their best work.

8.2 Challenges in Leading a Diverse Team.

There are several challenges that managers may face when leading a diverse team, including:

Communication issues: Different team members may have different communication styles, and managers need to be aware of and adapt to these differences.

Unconscious bias: Even with the best intentions, it is common for people to have unconscious biases that can affect how they perceive and interact with others. It is important for managers to be aware of their own biases and to work to minimize their impact.

Inclusion: Ensuring that all team members feel included and valued can be a challenge, especially if there are significant differences in backgrounds or experiences. It is important for managers to create an inclusive culture and to make an effort to understand and respect the perspectives of all team members.

8.3 Strategies for Leading a Diverse Team.

There are several strategies that managers can use to effectively lead and manage a diverse team, including:

Encouraging open communication: By creating an open and inclusive culture, managers can encourage team members to share their thoughts and ideas and foster a sense of collaboration.

Providing diversity training: Training can help to raise awareness of unconscious biases and promote inclusivity.

Creating a diverse hiring process: By actively seeking out and recruiting a diverse range of candidates, managers can create a more diverse team.

Promoting diversity and inclusion: Managers can promote diversity and inclusion by setting clear expectations and holding team members accountable for their behavior.

8.4 Conclusion

In summary, diversity and inclusion are crucial for the success of any organization. Leading a diverse team can present challenges, but it can also lead to better decision-making, increased creativity and innovation, and improved performance. By encouraging open communication, providing diversity training, creating a diverse hiring process, and promoting diversity and inclusion, managers can effectively lead and manage a diverse team.

Chapter Nine

Managing Change

In this chapter, we will discuss the importance of change management in organizations and explore strategies for successfully implementing change.

9.1 The Importance of Change Management.

Change is a constant in business, and organizations need to be able to adapt and respond to new challenges and opportunities. Change management is the process of planning and implementing change in an organization in a way that minimizes disruption and maximizes the chances of success.

9.2 Steps in the Change Management Process.

There are several steps involved in the change management process, including:

Identifying the need for change: The first step in change management is to identify the need for change. This may involve conducting a SWOT analysis or gathering feedback from team members.

Planning the change: Once the need for change has been identified, the next step is to create a plan for implementing it. This should include specific goals and objectives, a timeline, and a plan for allocating resources.

Communicating the change: It is important to communicate the change to all team members and stakeholders. This should include an explanation of the reasons for the change and the benefits it will bring.

Implementing the change: The next step is to put the change plan into action. This may involve training team members on new processes or procedures, updating systems, and technology, or making other necessary changes.

Monitoring progress: It is important to regularly monitor progress to ensure

Chapter Conclusion

Ethics and Social Responsibility

In this chapter, we will discuss the importance of ethical behavior and social responsibility in management and explore strategies for promoting these values within an organization.

10.1 The Importance of Ethics and Social Responsibility.

Ethical behavior and social responsibility are crucial for the success of any organization. Ethical behavior involves acting in a way that is fair, honest, and transparent, and that respects the rights and interests of all stakeholders. Social responsibility involves taking into account the impact of an organization's actions on society and the environment and taking steps to minimize any negative impacts.

10.2 Challenges in Promoting Ethics and Social Responsibility.

There are several challenges that managers may face when promoting ethics and social responsibility, including:

Conflicting values: Different team members or stakeholders may have different values, and it can be challenging to reconcile these differences.

Pressure to prioritize profits: In a competitive business environment, there may be pressure to prioritize profits over ethics and social responsibility.

Limited resources: It can be challenging to implement ethical and socially responsible practices if there are resource constraints.

10.3 Strategies for Promoting Ethics and Social Responsibility.

There are several strategies that managers can use to promote ethics and social responsibility within their organizations, including:

Setting clear expectations: By establishing clear guidelines and expectations for ethical behavior and social responsibility, managers can create a culture that values these principles.

Leading by example: Managers can promote ethical and socially responsible behaviors by modeling these behaviors themselves.

Providing training: Training can help to raise awareness of ethical and social responsibility issues and promote a culture of integrity.

Establishing a code of conduct: A code of conduct can help to set clear standards for ethical behavior and provide guidance to team members.

10.4 Conclusion

In summary, ethical behavior and social responsibility are crucial for the success of any organization. While there are challenges in promoting these values, managers can use strategies such as setting clear expectations, leading by example, providing training, and establishing a code of conduct to create a culture that values these principles.

www.ingramcontent.com/pod-product-compliance
Lightning Source LLC
Chambersburg PA
CBHW050323220526
45465CB00005B/2110